Ladybugs

Victoria Blakemore

Copyright info/picture credits

Cover, seecreateimages/AdobeStock; Page 3, torstensimon/ Pixabay; Page 5, makamuki0/Pixabay; Page 7, Myriams-Fotos/ Pixabay; Page 9, Alekss/Adobestock; Page 11, HypnoArt/ Pixabay; Pages 12-13, CCat82/AdobeStock; Page 15, kocsisa-nyi78/AdobeStock; Page 17, leoleobobeo/Pixabay; Page 19, olympus E5/AdobeStock; Page 21, 7monarda/Pixabay; Page 23; AngelaJMaher/Pixabay; Page 25, TheUjulala/Pixabay; Page 27, seecreateimages/AdobeStock; Page 29, Fix-iPixi_Deluxe/Pixabay; Page 31, mirena72i/Pixabay; Page 33, code83/Pixabay

Table of Contents

What are Ladybugs? 2

Kinds of Ladybugs 4

Physical Characteristics 6

Parts of a Ladybug 9

Habitat 10

Range 12

Diet 14

Self Defense 16

Movement 18

Ladybug Eggs 20

Ladybug Larvae 22

Ladybug Pupas 24

Adult Ladybugs 26

Population 28

Lucky Ladybugs 30

Helping Farmers 32

Glossary 34

What Are Ladybugs?

Ladybugs are small insects. They are also sometimes called "ladybirds" or "lady beetles."

Although they have the word "lady" in their name, not all ladybugs are girls.

Ladybugs are known for their

red body and black spots.

Kinds of Ladybugs

Most people think of ladybugs as red bugs with black spots. There are actually over 5,000 different kinds of ladybugs.

They can be red, orange, pink, brown, yellow, or black. Some ladybugs don't even have spots.

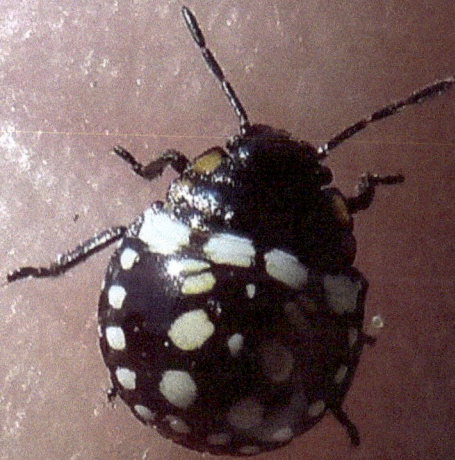

Harlequin ladybirds can be
many different colors. They
can also have different
patterns of spots.

5

Physical Characteristics

Like other insects, ladybugs

have six legs. They also have

a **segmented** body.

Ladybugs have a hard

shell-like part called an

elytra. Their wings are

underneath it. Their elytra is

the part of their body that

usually has spots.

A ladybug's wings are hidden

under the elytra until they fly.

Ladybugs have a **pronotum**.

It is right behind their head.

The pronotum protects the

ladybug's head.

The antennae are on the

ladybug's head. They are

used to smell, taste, and

touch. They help ladybugs

find their food.

Parts of a Ladybug

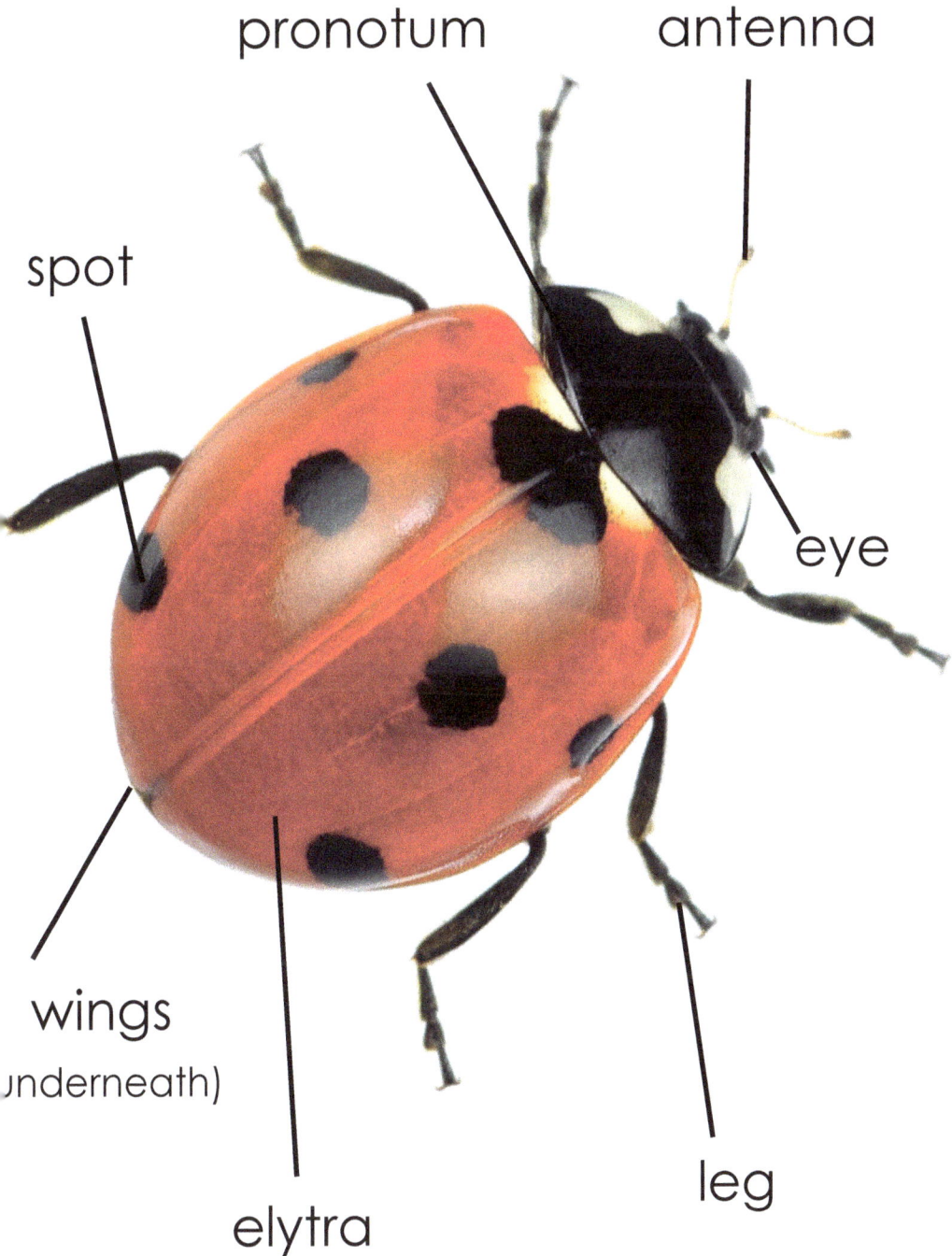

pronotum

antenna

spot

eye

wings
(underneath)

leg

elytra

Habitat

Ladybugs can live in many

different habitats. They

prefer areas that are warm

with lots of plants.

They are often found in fields

of crops, gardens, and

forests.

Range

Ladybugs are found on almost every continent. The only place they are not found is Antarctica.

In places where it gets very cold, ladybugs may **hibernate** for the winter.

Diet

Ladybugs are **insectivores**. They eat other insects. They are good to have in a garden because they eat bugs that eat plants.

Their diet is made up of aphids. Aphids are very small insects that feed on plants.

Aphids are pests. They eat

plants and can destroy

gardens and crops.

Self Defense

Ladybugs can be poisonous to animals. Their bright colors are warnings to animals that may want to eat them.

Ladybugs can release a bit of yellow blood when they are in danger. It has a bad smell and keeps animals away.

Ladybugs can tuck their legs

under their body and play

dead when a **predator** is near.

Movement

When ladybugs fly, their elytra opens up and their wings unfold. Ladybugs can fly up to fifteen miles per hour.

Ladybug wings move very fast. Their wings flap up to 85 times per second.

Ladybug Eggs

Ladybugs lay small, yellow eggs on the leaf of a plant. They usually lay their eggs under the leaf. This makes it harder for predators to find them.

Ladybugs can lay up to 1,000 eggs in their lifetime!

Ladybugs often lay their

eggs in the summer.

Ladybug Larvae

When the eggs hatch, the young ladybugs that come out are called **larvae**.

The larvae are usually black with bright stripes or spots. Ladybug larvae have spikes along their body.

Larvae eat a lot of insects. They
have to get ready to become a
pupa.

Ladybug Pupas

After a few days, each larva will curl up and form a hard covering. At this time, they are called **pupas**.

After a few days, the adult ladybugs will come out.

The hard covering protects the pupa as it **transforms** into an adult ladybug.

Adult Ladybugs

When ladybugs first come out of the pupa, their elytra is soft. It takes a few hours to harden. As it hardens, the color of the elytra becomes brighter.

Like many insects, ladybugs do not live for long. Many ladybugs live for about one year.

Population

In many places, there are fewer ladybugs than there used to be. This is a problem for farmers.

People are trying to help ladybugs. They are keeping track of where ladybugs are found. They are also releasing more ladybugs into the wild.

Lucky Ladybugs

In many places, ladybugs are thought to be lucky. This is because they eat insects that eat crops.

Some people believe that a ladybug brings good luck if it lands on you.

Don't brush a ladybug off if it lands on you. It might bring you good luck!

Helping Farmers

Ladybugs are good to have in your garden because they stop aphids from eating your plants.

Some farmers release ladybugs in their fields to protect their crops from insects like aphids.

Glossary

Elytra: the hard outer shell of a ladybug

Hibernate: to sleep through the winter when less food is available

Insectivore: an animal that eats only insects

Larva: an insect after it hatches from an egg

Predator: an animal that hunts other creatures for food

Pronotum: the hard, round part of a ladybug's body that protects the head

Pupa: the stage of a ladybug's life cycle when they are in a hard shell and growing into an adult

Segmented: separated into parts

Transform: to change

About the Author

Victoria Blakemore is a first grade

teacher in Southwest Florida with a

passion for reading.

You can visit her at

www.elementaryexplorers.com

Also in This Series

Elementary Explorers **Gray Wolves**	Elementary Explorers **Sloths**	Elementary Explorers **Flamingos**	Elementary Explorers **Camels**	Elementary Explorers **Koalas**	Elementary Explorers **Honey Bees**
Victoria Blakemore	Victoria Blakemore	Victoria Blakemore	Victoria Blakemore	Victoria Blakemore	Victoria Blakemore
Elementary Explorers **Pandas**	Elementary Explorers **Pangolins**	Elementary Explorers **White-Tailed Deer**	Elementary Explorers **Orcas**	Elementary Explorers **Giraffes**	Elementary Explorers **Corn**
Victoria Blakemore	Victoria Blakemore	Victoria Blakemore	Victoria Blakemore	Victoria Blakemore	Victoria Blakemore
Elementary Explorers **Meerkats**	Elementary Explorers **Echidnas**	Elementary Explorers **Walruses**	Elementary Explorers **Raccoons**	Elementary Explorers **Bald Eagles**	Elementary Explorers **Apples**
Victoria Blakemore	Victoria Blakemore	Victoria Blakemore	Victoria Blakemore	Victoria Blakemore	Victoria Blakemore
Elementary Explorers **Arctic Foxes**	Elementary Explorers **Red Pandas**	Elementary Explorers **Cassowaries**	Elementary Explorers **Tigers**	Elementary Explorers **Ladybugs**	Elementary Explorers **Moose**
Victoria Blakemore	Victoria Blakemore	Victoria Blakemore	Victoria Blakemore	Victoria Blakemore	Victoria Blakemore
Elementary Explorers **Beluga Whales**	Elementary Explorers **Leopards**	Elementary Explorers **Elephants**	Elementary Explorers **Jellyfish**	Elementary Explorers **Binturongs**	Elementary Explorers **Lions**
Victoria Blakemore	Victoria Blakemore	Victoria Blakemore	Victoria Blakemore	Victoria Blakemore	Victoria Blakemore
Elementary Explorers **Dolphins**	Elementary Explorers **Reindeer**	Elementary Explorers **Hammerhead Sharks**	Elementary Explorers **Hippos**	Elementary Explorers **Pumpkins**	Elementary Explorers **Peafowl**
Victoria Blakemore	Victoria Blakemore	Victoria Blakemore	Victoria Blakemore	Victoria Blakemore	Victoria Blakemore

Also in This Series

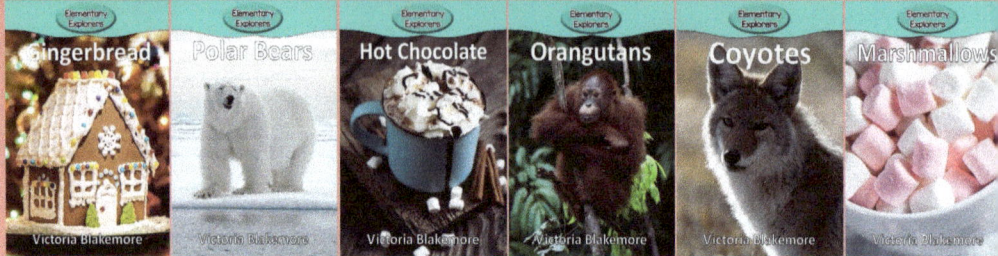

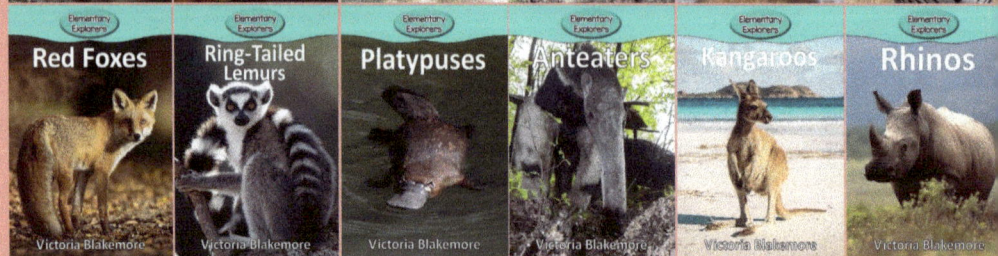

Chameleons Victoria Blakemore	**Florida Panthers** Victoria Blakemore	**Aye-Ayes** Victoria Blakemore	**Black Bears** Victoria Blakemore	**Cheetahs** Victoria Blakemore	**Manatees** Victoria Blakemore
Gingerbread Victoria Blakemore	**Polar Bears** Victoria Blakemore	**Hot Chocolate** Victoria Blakemore	**Orangutans** Victoria Blakemore	**Coyotes** Victoria Blakemore	**Marshmallows** Victoria Blakemore
Strawberries Victoria Blakemore	**Aardvarks** Victoria Blakemore	**Mako Sharks** Victoria Blakemore	**Alligators** Victoria Blakemore	**Frogs** Victoria Blakemore	**Hedgehogs** Victoria Blakemore
Brown Bears Victoria Blakemore	**Bongos** Victoria Blakemore	**Sea Turtles** Victoria Blakemore	**Quokkas** Victoria Blakemore	**Muskrats** Victoria Blakemore	**Zebras** Victoria Blakemore
Red Foxes Victoria Blakemore	**Ring-Tailed Lemurs** Victoria Blakemore	**Platypuses** Victoria Blakemore	**Anteaters** Victoria Blakemore	**Kangaroos** Victoria Blakemore	**Rhinos** Victoria Blakemore
Jaguars Victoria Blakemore	**Wombats** Victoria Blakemore				

www.ingramcontent.com/pod-product-compliance
Lightning Source LLC
Chambersburg PA
CBHW051252020426
42333CB00025B/3173